ALFALFA HILL

ALFALFA HILL

WRITTEN AND ILLUSTRATED BY PETER PARNALL

DOUBLEDAY & COMPANY, INC., GARDEN CITY, NEW YORK

Library of Congress Cataloging in Publication Data

Parnall, Peter
   Alfalfa Hill
   SUMMARY: Describes the coming of winter and its
effect on the animal inhabitants of a New Jersey hill.
   [1. Winter—Fiction] I. Title.
PZ7.P243Al   [E]
ISBN 0-385-02448-7 Trade
        0-385-02200-X Prebound
Library of Congress Catalog Card Number 74-186

FOR THE CHILDREN ON ALL THE HILLS

The wind howled over Alfalfa Hill.
It ripped crisp leaves from the whipping trees
And hurled them crazily, crazily.
They crackled and scraped and nestled,
Covering the forest floor.

Warm air went and cold air came.
The robins were gone,
But the mockingbird stayed
Guarding his place in the wild rose bush.

The squirrels skittered from rock to stump
Gathering acorns, black walnuts, and tulip tree seeds.
They buried their hoards beneath the leaves
And now and then in a hollow tree.

Deer browsed on honeysuckle leaves
That still hung green in the frigid air.
Grouse leaped high for frozen clumps of dried wild grapes,
And mice raced for seeds where rotten apples used to lie.

The old fat coon knew what was coming
And he ate and he ate, and he ate and he ate
Berries and nuts, bugs and corn,
Apples and frogs, and . . . it came . . .   Whisper.

The snow.

Quiet, quiet it drifted down.
No whoosh, no sound.
No warning at all . . . Whisper.
Hour after hour it fell.

Like a world full of cotton it muffled all sound.

Deeper and deeper it whispered, whispered,

Making caves of viny honeysuckle clumps.

All night long the white blanket grew thicker and thicker.

The screech owl peered from his woody den
And stayed home from his evening hunt.

When the sun's first rays struck Alfalfa Hill
The creatures were wondering.

They were looking.

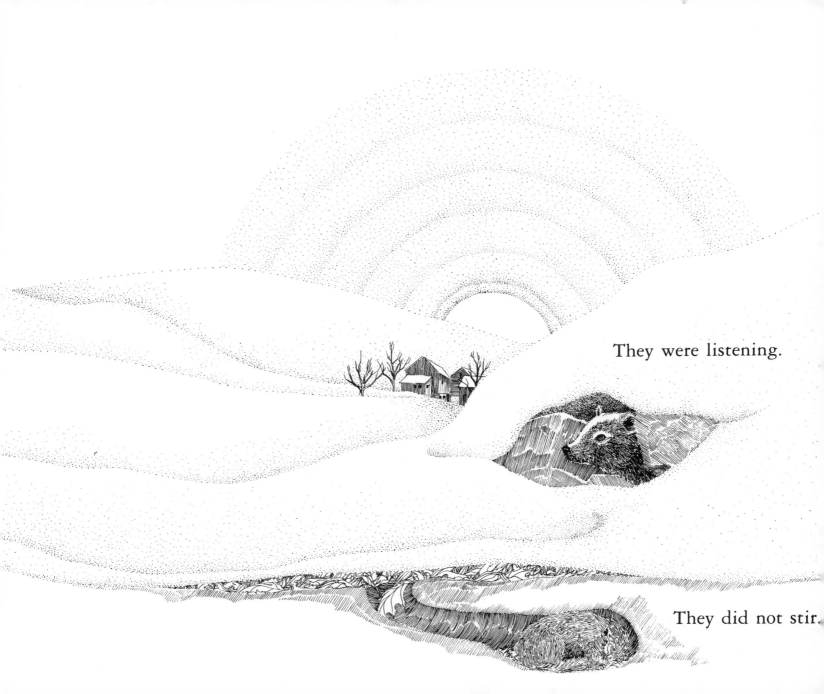

They were listening.

They did not stir.

No more rocky hedgerows wandering through the woods,
No more masses of tangled vines.
No green spruces reaching for the sky.
Now giant white mushrooms met the eye.
Ghosts, and marshmallows.

The air was still.
There were no squeaks, no chatters, no peeps or clucks.
No rustling, scratching, chewing, or caws . . .
No preening, combing, or washing one's paws.

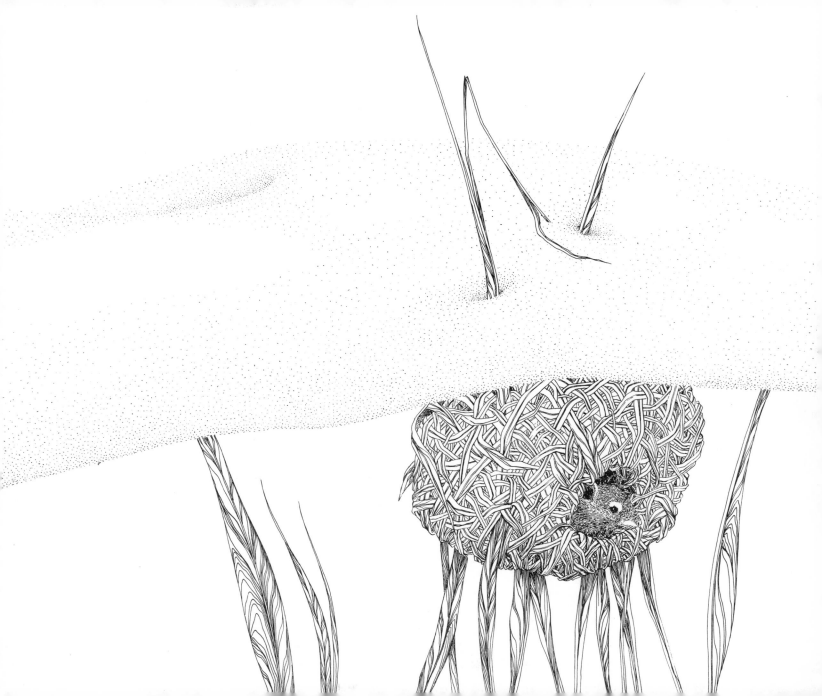

The birds sat silently and watched their new world.

Winter.

A dangerous time for some
Whose color no longer matches the forest floor.
Beware, little mouse,
You are far from home.
Quiet is the word for winter.
Look and listen before you leap.
Find your food as fast as you can

And run home on silent feet.

PETER PARNALL has always loved the land and the creatures that inhabit it. During part of his childhood he lived in a desert, where there were more wild things than children for playmates.

A desire to return to the country prompted him to leave the advertising business in New York and settle with his family on a farm in the Delaware Valley. An intense interest in conservation motivates more and more of his activities. Among the products of his concern are *The Great Fish,* a fable about a heritage we have all but lost, *The Mountain,* a comment on national parks, and *The Nightwatchers,* a personal look at American owls.

Mr. Parnall has illustrated over two dozen books, several of which have appeared on the New York *Times* Best-Illustrated list. His work has also won acclaim from the American Institute of Graphic Arts. In addition to writing and illustrating, he teaches at Lafayette College.